A Closer Look at

GENES AND GENETIC ENGINEERING

INTRODUCTION TO BIOLOGY

A Closer Look at GENES AND GENETIC ENGINEERING

Edited By Michael Anderson

Britannica®
Educational Publishing

IN ASSOCIATION WITH

ROSEN
EDUCATIONAL SERVICES

Published in 2012 by Britannica Educational Publishing
(a trademark of Encyclopædia Britannica, Inc.)
in association with Rosen Educational Services, LLC
29 East 21st Street, New York, NY 10010.

First Edition

Britannica Educational Publishing
Michael I. Levy: Executive Editor, Encyclopædia Britannica
J.E. Luebering: Director, Core Reference Group, Encyclopædia Britannica
Adam Augustyn: Assistant Manager, Encyclopædia Britannica

Anthony L. Green: Editor, Compton's by Britannica
Michael Anderson: Senior Editor, Compton's by Britannica
Sherman Hollar: Associate Editor, Compton's by Britannica

Marilyn L. Barton: Senior Coordinator, Production Control
Steven Bosco: Director, Editorial Technologies
Lisa S. Braucher: Senior Producer and Data Editor
Yvette Charboneau: Senior Copy Editor
Kathy Nakamura: Manager, Media Acquisition

Rosen Educational Services
Heather M. Moore Niver: Editor
Nelson Sá: Art Director
Cindy Reiman: Photography Manager
Karen Huang: Photo Researcher
Matthew Cauli: Designer, Cover Design
Introduction by Heather M. Moore Niver

Library of Congress Cataloging-in-Publication Data

A closer look at genes and genetic engineering / edited by Michael Anderson.
    p. cm.—(Introduction to biology)
"In association with Britannica Educational Publishing, Rosen Educational Services."
Includes bibliographical references and index.
ISBN 978-1-61530-527-8 (library binding)
1. Genes—Juvenile literature. 2. Genetic engineering—Juvenile literature. I. Anderson, Michael
(Michael J.), 1972-
QH447.C56 2012
572.8'6—dc22

                                                                                    2011007581

Manufactured in the United States of America

On the cover: A chromosome is a microscopic, threadlike part of the cell that carries hereditary information in the form of genes. *Shutterstock.com*

On the cover (background), back cover, page 3: DNA strands. *Adrian Neal/Lifesize/Getty Images*

Pages 12, 32, 44, 54, 63, 77, 78, 81, 84, 85 © www.istockphoto.com/uzinusa; pp. 19, 34, 41, 42, 43, 46, 47, 51, 52, 56, 74, 75 © www.istockphoto.com/penfold; remaining interior background image © www.istockphoto.com/Osuleo

CONTENTS

Maybe you know someone who is the spitting image of someone else in the family. This is thanks to genes. Genetics, the study of genes, involves far more than family resemblances, though. A century after pioneering experiments revealed the role of genes in heredity, scientists learned that genetic engineering—the manipulation of genes—can be an important tool in medicine and agriculture. This book provides an overview of the history of genetics. It offers an explanation of how genes work as well as what can happen when genetic defects occur. It also explores some up-and-coming technologies that harness the power of genetic engineering.

People have known since ancient times that particular traits can be passed along from parent to offspring. How this occurred was long a mystery, though. Scientists proposed many theories through the years. One prevailing theory of the early 1800s was blending inheritance, which held that an organism's heritable traits are a combination of those in the parents. Charles Darwin used this theory to support his own theory of natural selection.

In the mid-1800s an Austrian monk named Gregor Mendel became the first person to show scientifically how specific characteristics pass from one generation to the next. Experimenting with garden peas, Mendel deduced that distinct hereditary units that passed from parent to offspring determined how traits were inherited. These units eventually became known as genes. By studying the humble pea plant, Mendel was able to demonstrate fundamental genetic principles such as segregation and independent assortment.

Biologists who followed in Mendel's footsteps discovered how genes and chromosomes were related and, eventually, the role of DNA. In the early 1900s Thomas H. Morgan determined that genes are found on chromosomes, with each gene located at a specific site, and that patterns of inheritance are based on the position of genes on each chromosome. Morgan also verified that genes near one another on the same chromosome are apt to be inherited together.

Chromosomes are a collection of DNA and protein found in every living thing. Each gene has a specific place on a specific chromosome. Most organisms have two sets of

In the United States, most commercially grown corn is genetically modified. Adam Gault/OJO Images/Getty Images

paired chromosomes, with one set inherited from each parent. When cells reproduce, chromosomes carry genetic information from the parent cell to the newly produced daughter cells. Most cells reproduce through a process called mitosis. In mitosis one cell divides into two exact copies of itself. But gametes (sex cells) duplicate through meiosis, which involves two cell divisions. The first division produces two daughter cells with a full set of chromosomes. In the second division, however, the chromosomes do not duplicate, resulting in four daughter cells with only half as many chromosomes. The full set of chromosomes is restored when

a male gamete, or sperm, combines with a female gamete, or egg, during fertilization.

When defects occur in the genetic material, diseases known as genetic disorders result. The cause can be mutations, or alterations in the DNA sequence, of a single gene or defects in an entire chromosome. Single-gene disorders result from one or more mutations in a single gene that prevent it from acting properly. Chromosome disorders occur from structural defects in a chromosome or from having too many or too few chromosomes. Down's syndrome, for example, arises in people with an extra chromosome 21.

Genetic engineering involves the artificial manipulation of genes to change an organism. Biologists first began experimenting with this process in the 1960s. Initially, genetic engineering referred to any method used for modifying organisms though heredity and reproduction. This included artificial insemination and selective breeding. In modern science, however, the term refers specifically to the field of recombinant DNA technology. In this process, DNA from at least two sources is combined and then inserted into a host organism. There, the inserted DNA replicates and functions along with the DNA of the host.

Although some people worry that genetic engineering could have dangerous consequences, others tout its benefits, including the creation of safer vaccines. This debate will undoubtedly continue. Nevertheless, genetic engineering will remain an essential focus of genetics, and further study will only expand its uses in agriculture, medicine, and other areas.

CHAPTER 1

GENETICS: THE STUDY OF GENES

Why do offspring resemble their parents? Such resemblances are passed on relatively unaltered from generation to generation through a process called heredity. The units of heredity are genes, which are made up

Children look like their parents because genes are passed on from one generation to the next, a process called heredity. iStockphoto/ Thinkstock

of deoxyribonucleic acid (DNA). Genes are found on chromosomes, which are threadlike parts inside every cell. Encoded in every gene are biochemical instructions that determine the characteristics, or traits, of an organism. Genetics is the study of genes—how they operate and how they are transmitted from parents to offspring.

EARLY THEORIES OF HEREDITY

Even before the beginnings of written history people were aware that certain traits could be passed from parent to offspring. By selectively breeding animals or plants, humans produced livestock and crops that could provide food, pull plows, and supply companionship and protection. But while farmers and breeders learned to control the transmission of traits in agriculture, the actual process of heredity remained a mystery. Many theories were advanced. In ancient Greece, it was thought that traits were transmitted through the blood, and the word *blood* is still often used to denote ancestry. In the 17th century, some biologists held that female eggs contained miniature offspring, with male sperm merely triggering embryonic development. Other biologists proposed the opposite—that tiny

ON

THE ORIGIN OF SPECIES

BY MEANS OF NATURAL SELECTION,

OR THE

PRESERVATION OF FAVOURED RACES IN THE STRUGGLE FOR LIFE.

By CHARLES DARWIN, M.A.,

FELLOW OF THE ROYAL, GEOLOGICAL, LINNÆAN, ETC., SOCIETIES;
AUTHOR OF 'JOURNAL OF RESEARCHES DURING H. M. S. BEAGLE'S VOYAGE
ROUND THE WORLD.'

LONDON:
JOHN MURRAY, ALBEMARLE STREET.
1859.

The right of Translation is reserved.

but fully formed offspring were present in the sperm.

By the 19th century, three theories on heredity prevailed within the scientific community: pangenesis, acquired characteristics, and blending inheritance. Pangenesis held that every cell produced gemmules, particles that embodied the cell's traits and that coalesced in the reproductive organs to form offspring. The theory of acquired characteristics stated that traits acquired during an organism's life, such as increased muscle from exercise, were passed on to offspring. Blending inheritance proposed that an organism's heritable characteristics are a blend of those in the parents. For example, offspring of a tall plant and short plant would be of medium height.

In his 1859 book *On the Origin of Species*, English biologist Charles Darwin cited blending inheritance as a possible explanation for the variation observed in nature. Variation in traits played a key role in Darwin's theory of

In his book On the Origin of Species, *Charles Darwin proposed that blending inheritance could be a reason for variations in nature.* **SSPL via Getty Images**

natural selection. Darwin observed that species produce more offspring than can survive, given Earth's limited resources. Individuals with traits providing an advantage in their surroundings are more likely to survive and reproduce than individuals lacking these characteristics. If the environment changes, species with traits that are adaptive in the new circumstances will survive. Those lacking such adaptations may become extinct.

Darwin did not know what controlled heredity or how traits passed to offspring. However, he knew that for natural selection to operate, there had to be variable units of heredity, and that variations in species arose through the accumulation of changes in these units over time. Darwin later revived interest in pangenesis, thinking that it explained what he had observed. Unknown to Darwin, a study of inheritance already under way would soon provide a conclusive explanation for the mysteries of inheritance.

GREGOR MENDEL — PIONEER OF CLASSICAL GENETICS

In 1865 Gregor Mendel, an Austrian monk, wrote a paper that laid the foundation for modern genetics. Mendel was the first to

Gregor Mendel. Hulton Archive/Getty Images

demonstrate experimentally the manner in which specific traits are passed from one generation to the next and to use mathematics to analyze his data. He concluded that discrete, or distinct, hereditary units that passed from parent to offspring determined how traits were inherited. Mendel's findings were ahead of his time—their significance, and the hereditary elements he described, were not understood until the early 1900s, when the units became known as genes.

In the monastery garden where he conducted his experiments, Mendel used the garden pea, *Pisum sativum*, as his model organism. The plant is ideal genetic working material: it is easily raised and produces many progeny in a short time. The plants are self-fertilizing, and their reproductive anatomy prevents accidental outside fertilization. This allowed Mendel to control which plants were bred.

Principle of Segregation

Mendel examined seven traits that each had two distinct forms in pea plants. He first studied the inheritance of one trait at a time. This is called a monohybrid cross. To study petal color, he chose purebred purple

MENDEL'S LIFE

Johann Mendel was born on July 22, 1822, in Heinzendorf, Austria. He took the name Gregor when he entered the monastery in Brünn, Moravia (now Brno, Czech Republic), in 1843. He studied for two years at the Philosophical Institute in Olmütz (now Olomouc, Czech Republic), before going to Brünn. He became a priest in 1847. For most of the next 20 years he taught at a nearby high school, except for two years of study at the University of Vienna (1851–53). In 1868 Mendel was elected abbot of the monastery.

Mendel's famous garden-pea experiments began in 1856 in the monastery garden. He proposed that the existence of characteristics such as blossom color is caused by the occurrence of paired elementary units of heredity, now known as genes. Mendel presented his work to the local natural science society in 1865 in a paper entitled "Experiments with Plant Hybrids." Administrative duties after 1868 kept him too busy for further research, so he lived out his life in relative obscurity. Mendel died on Jan. 6, 1884. In 1900 independent research by other scientists confirmed Mendel's results.

flowers and purebred white flowers for the parental, or P generation. When these were crossed, all their offspring—labeled the F_1 (first filial) generation—had purple flowers. Mendel crossed the F_1 plants with each other to produce an F_2 (second filial) generation. Roughly 75 percent of the F_2 flowers had purple flowers, and the remaining 25 percent had white petals. When Mendel replicated this procedure with other traits, each cross produced the same pattern: one parental trait was expressed in all of the F_1 generation and in 75 percent of the F_2 generation; the remaining F_2 generation displayed the nondominant trait.

Mendel analyzed his results using probability theory. He concluded that each plant had two factors for a given trait—one factor was inherited from each parent plant. Each parent had two factors for the trait, but during reproduction the factors segregated, or separated from each other. One factor of each pair was transmitted to each offspring. Which offspring received which factor of the pair was a matter of chance. Mendel called this the principle of segregation.

Today the factors Mendel described are called alleles. A pair of alleles—one from each parent—makes up a gene. The expressed characteristic of a gene (flower color, for example) is called the phenotype. The allele combination (identical alleles versus different alleles) for each trait is the genotype.

Using a grid called a Punnett square helps diagram the probability of each possible phenotype and genotype in a generation. Let R stand for the allele for purple flower color and r for the white petal allele. For many traits one allele form is dominant to the other: if the dominant allele is present, the dominant phenotype is expressed regardless of whether the second allele is the same (RR) or the alternative form (Rr). The nondominant form of the allele is called recessive. The recessive phenotype is expressed only when both alleles in the gene pair are the recessive form (rr).

The allele combination for each trait is the genotype. If the two alleles are alike—RR or rr—the genotype is described as homozygous. If the alleles are different—for example, Rr—the genotype is called heterozygous.

In a monohybrid cross beginning with a P generation of homozygous dominants (RR) and homozygous recessives (rr), all members of the F_I generation display the dominant

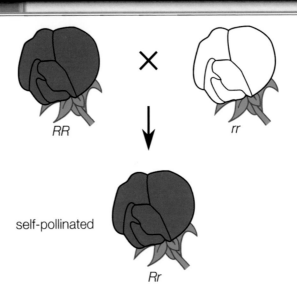

parental generation (P)

self-pollinated

F_1 generation

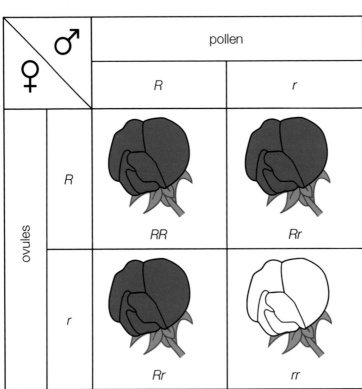

F_2 generation

phenotype (purple) but have a heterozygous genotype (*Rr*). A cross of two F$_1$ individuals (*Rr* × *Rr*) produces an F$_2$ generation composed of both dominant phenotypes and recessive phenotypes in an approximately 3:1 ratio—roughly 75 percent of the F$_2$ will have purple flowers, and 25 percent will display white flowers. The genotypic ratio of the F$_2$ is 1:2:1—roughly 25 percent homozygous dominant (*RR*), 50 percent heterozygous (*Rr*), and 25 percent homozygous recessive (*rr*) individuals.

PRINCIPLE OF INDEPENDENT ASSORTMENT

Using the same basic procedure as for a monohybrid cross, Mendel next studied the simultaneous inheritance of two traits—a dihybrid cross. He wanted to see if the factors for two different traits segregated independently of each other during gamete formation. When he crossed pure strains displaying yellow, smooth seeds (*AABB*) with

> *Mendel's principle of segregation states that during gamete formation the alleles in each gene segregate and pass randomly into gametes. In a monohybrid cross, the F$_2$ generation displays two phenotypes in a 3:1 ratio.* Encyclopædia Britannica, Inc.

Principle of Independent Assortment

 AABB ×   aabb

parental generation (P)

self-pollinated   AaBb

F₁ generation

	♂ pollen			
♀	AB	Ab	aB	ab
AB	AABB	AABb	AaBB	AaBb
Ab	AABb	AAbb	AaBb	Aabb
aB	AaBB	AaBb	aaBB	aaBb
ab	AaBb	Aabb	aaBb	aabb

ovules

F₂ generation

Mendel's principle of independent assortment states that during gamete formation the alleles in one gene segregate and pass into gametes independently of the alleles in other genes. In a dihybrid cross, the F₂ generation will display four phenotypes in a 9:3:3:1 ratio. **Encyclopædia Britannica, Inc.**

strains that had green, wrinkled seeds (*aabb*), all of the F_1 generation were heterozygotes with smooth yellow seeds (*AaBb*). The F_2 generation displayed four phenotypes—smooth yellow, smooth green, wrinkled yellow, and wrinkled green—in a 9:3:3:1 ratio.

These results showed that segregation of color alleles (*A* and *a*) was independent of segregation of the alleles for seed shape (*B* and *b*). The *A* allele may assort with *B* or *b*, and the *a* allele may assort with *B* or *b*. This means that one trait (such as color) may display the dominant form while the other trait (seed shape) may be dominant or recessive, and vice versa. For example, wrinkled yellow peas (*Aabb* or *AAbb*) are dominant for color but recessive for seed shape; the reverse is seen for smooth green peas (*aaBb* or *aaBB*). Mendel called this the principle of independent assortment.

Because of independent assortment, F_1 individuals in a dihybrid cross produce four possible allele combinations: *AB*, *Ab*, *aB*, and *ab*. Random union during fertilization produces the four observed phenotypes in a 9:3:3:1 ratio and nine different genotypes: *AABB*, *AABb*, *AAbb*, *AaBB*, *AaBb*, *Aabb*, *aaBB*, *aaBb*, and *aabb*.

Non-Mendelian Inheritance

Traits that are inherited according to Mendel's principles are called Mendelian traits. However, most traits are non-Mendelian, meaning that they display different patterns of inheritance.

Incomplete Dominance

When red-flowered and white-flowered snapdragons or impatiens are crossed, the F_1 displays pink flowers—an intermediate phenotype. This occurs not from blending, but because the red allele in these flowers shows incomplete dominance: the F_1 has an intermediate phenotype but carries both the dominant and recessive alleles. Unlike blending inheritance, a cross of F_1

Breeding genetically dominant red impatiens with genetically recessive white impatiens produces hybrid offspring with pink flowers. Shutterstock.com

heterozygotes produces an F_2 of red, pink, and white flowers in a 1:2:1 ratio.

CODOMINANCE

In codominance, the heterozygote displays the phenotypic characteristics of both alleles. An example of a codominant trait is the MN blood group system of human beings. Blood type in the MN system is determined by the alleles M and N. Homozygotes for the M allele (MM) have a particular molecule on the surface of their red blood cells. Those individuals homozygous for the N blood type (NN) carry a different surface molecule. Heterozygotes (MN) carry both surface proteins: the M and the N.

LINKAGE AND CROSSING OVER

During meiosis—the type of cell division that produces sex cells—homologous chromosomes (those having the same kind of genes) exchange some of their genes. This is called crossing over, or recombination. In most cases, crossing over is beneficial. It increases genetic variation, which in turn can introduce phenotypes that may give the individual a physical or even evolutionary

Crossing Over During Meiosis

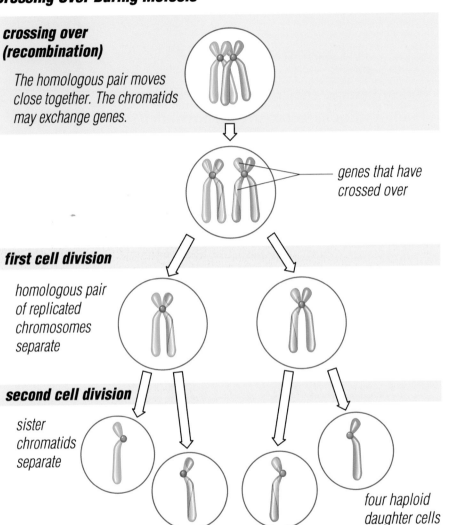

crossing over (recombination)

The homologous pair moves close together. The chromatids may exchange genes.

genes that have crossed over

first cell division

homologous pair of replicated chromosomes separate

second cell division

sister chromatids separate

four haploid daughter cells

Crossing over, or recombination, occurs in the early stages of meiosis, when the homologous pairs of replicated chromosomes are in close proximity. In most cases, crossing over is beneficial because it increases genetic variation in offspring. Encyclopædia Britannica, Inc.

advantage. Geneticists began to investigate crossing over when they noted that some inherited traits did not assort independently. For example, crosses between *AaBb* and *aabb* parents did not always produce the progeny—*AaBb, aaBb, Aabb,* and *aabb*— predicted by Mendel's principle. Instead, geneticists observed a greater number of the parental types (*AaBb* and *aabb*) and a smaller number of the recombinant types (*Aabb* and *aaBb*). Further study revealed that the dominant alleles of each gene were linked—they were situated so close to each other on one homolog that they were inherited together. The same held true for the recessive alleles on the other homolog. If this linkage were unbreakable, in meiosis the hybrid *AaBb* would form only *AB* and *ab* gametes. In fact, however, *Ab* and *aB* gametes were also formed—strong evidence that an exchange took place. (For a more detailed discussion of sex cells and meiosis, see Chapter 2.)

SEX LINKAGE

Traits determined by genes on the sex chromosomes are called sex-linked traits. Despite their location and name, most sex-linked

traits are not associated with gender-specific characteristics such as facial hair, but rather control inheritance of a wide range of characteristics.

In humans, a woman has two X chromosomes and 44 autosomes in each body cell and one X chromosome and 22 autosomes in each egg. A man carries one X and one Y chromosome and 44 autosomes in each body cell and either an X or a Y chromosome and 22 autosomes in each sperm cell. Most sex-linked traits result from genes located on the X chromosome. Few genes have been identified on the Y chromosome. Because of this, some people refer to sex-linked traits as X-linked traits.

Sex-linked traits may be recessive or dominant. Recessive sex-linked traits occur more frequently in men because males have no allele on the Y chromosome to counteract the effects of a recessive allele on the X chromosome. The genotype of these males is called hemizygous. The female must inherit the recessive allele on both of her X chromosomes to fully display the trait. Common examples of sex-linked recessive traits in humans include hemophilia, certain patterns of baldness, and color blindness.

POLYGENIC TRAITS AND MULTIFACTORIAL INHERITANCE

The expression of most traits results from the interaction of several genes and with environmental factors such as nutrition. Traits affected by more than one gene are sometimes called polygenic traits. Because their expression is affected by many factors, they are said to follow a multifactorial pattern of inheritance. Common examples include height and hair color in humans, coat color in dogs and other animals, milk yield in cattle, egg-laying capacity in poultry, and immune system function in all mammals.

CHAPTER 2

THE NATURE OF CHROMOSOMES AND GENES

Genes are located on chromosomes—tiny, threadlike structures inside the cells of every organism. Building on Mendel's pioneering work, biologists of the early 1900s discovered the relationship between genes and chromosomes. Later research revealed the essential role of DNA in inheritance.

THE DISCOVERY OF CHROMOSOMES

Chromosomes were discovered after Mendel's work was published. By the 1880s German biologist August Weismann had suggested that heredity depends on a special material called germ plasma located in the chromosomes that is transmitted unaltered from one generation to another. In 1902 American biologist Walter Sutton and German biologist Theodor Boveri independently established that chromosomes followed Mendel's principles. Using the grasshopper as his model organism, Sutton observed that chromosomes occurred in pairs and segregated and assorted independently during gamete formation. Boveri made the same observations with sea urchins. Based on their findings, the scientists also proposed that the factors (alleles) Mendel had discussed were located on chromosomes.

The discoveries of Sutton and Boveri laid the groundwork for the chromosome theory of inheritance. Formally proposed in 1910 by American geneticist Thomas H. Morgan, the theory confirms that genes are located on chromosomes, with each gene situated at a particular site, and that

By studying grasshoppers, Walter Sutton discovered that chromosomes occur in pairs but segregate and assort separately in the course of gamete formation. Shutterstock.com

GENETIC RESEARCH
SINCE THE MID-1900S

The work of the early geneticists provided a strong foundation for the great advances in genetics seen in the second half of the 20th century. The chemical makeup of genes and chromosomes had long been a mystery until 1944, when Oswald Avery discovered that DNA was the basic genetic material of the cell. The molecular structure of DNA was determined in 1953 by James Watson of the United States and Francis Crick of England. French geneticists François Jacob and Jacques Monod later determined how DNA directs protein synthesis, thereby deciphering the genetic code of the DNA molecule. Scientists working on the Human Genome Project, a study completed in 2003 that had been 13 years in the making, determined the DNA sequence of the three billion base pairs in human DNA and identified the almost 25,000 genes in the human genome.

James Watson and Francis Crick, shown here in a 1976 issue of National Geographic *magazine, discovered the molecular structure of DNA in 1953.* Ned M. Seidler/National Geographic Image Collection/Getty Image

patterns of inheritance can be explained by the location of genes on each chromosome. Using the fruit fly as his model organism, Morgan determined that genes located on the sex chromosomes had a unique pattern of inheritance, which he termed sex linkage. Morgan also confirmed the findings of earlier studies showing that genes lying close together on the same chromosome tend to be inherited together.

CHROMOSOMES AND CELL DIVISION

Chromosomes are aggregates of DNA and protein found in every living thing. Every gene has a specific location on a particular chromosome. Most organisms have two sets of paired chromosomes (the diploid number), with one set (the haploid number) inherited from each parent. Each chromosome pair consists of two homologs—chromosomes that resemble each other in both appearance and genetic characteristics—and each homolog has one allele of each gene pair. By convention, the haploid number of any species is designated by n, and the diploid number by xn, where x equals the number of chromosome sets.

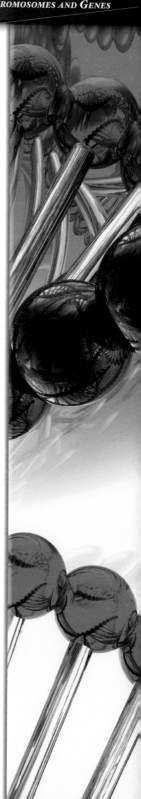

Some species can have three or more chromosome sets; this is called polyploidy. Specifically, polyploids are described by their number of chromosome sets — triploid (three sets), tetraploid (four sets), and so forth. Polyploidy is found in some animals, including goldfish and some salamanders, and most commonly in plants, including ferns, wheat, pansies, and many others. Humans are diploid; each somatic cell has a set of 23 chromosomes from each parent, for a total of 46. In humans, the haploid number (n) is 23, and the diploid number ($2n$) is 46.

"Mitosis is the process in which one cell divides into two identical cells. In the stage of mitosis called anaphase, two indentical sets of chromosomes are pulled to opposite ends of the cell that is about to divide." **Jupiterimages/Photos.com/Thinkstock**

MITOSIS

Unicellular organisms such as bacteria and the somatic cells of higher organisms replicate through mitosis, a process in which one cell gives rise to two genetically identical daughter cells. The chromosomes make exact copies of themselves, after which the duplicate sets separate as the cell divides, with one full set of chromosomes going into each of the two daughter cells. Each daughter cell acquires a full diploid set of chromosomes. This process is repeated every time cells divide.

MEIOSIS

Gamete formation occurs through a form of cell division called meiosis. During this process, the amount of hereditary material present in the gametes is reduced by half. Meiosis consists of two divisions. In the first division, the homologous chromosomes pair up and duplicate themselves, then each pair moves away from the other as the cell divides, producing two daughter cells, each with a diploid chromosome set. The daughter cells undergo a second division similar to mitosis, during which the chromosomes do not duplicate but merely separate. The

Meiosis Overview

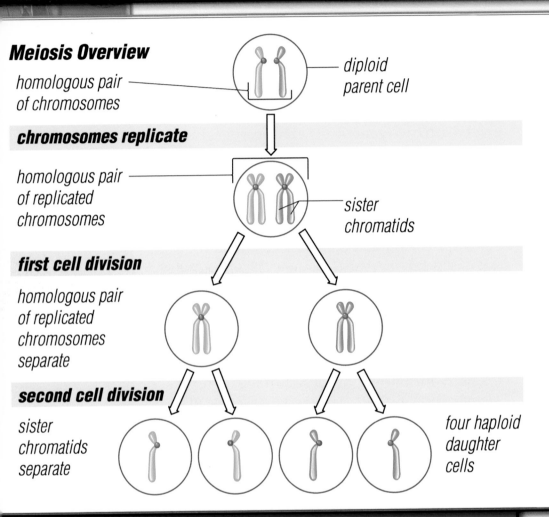

homologous pair
of chromosomes

diploid
parent cell

chromosomes replicate

homologous pair
of replicated
chromosomes

sister
chromatids

first cell division

homologous pair
of replicated
chromosomes
separate

second cell division

sister
chromatids
separate

four haploid
daughter
cells

A homologous pair of chromosomes consists of one chromosome from each parent. During most of the cell cycle, homologous chromosome pairs are unreplicated. When the chromosomes replicate, each chromosome of the pair becomes doubled. Each "half" of the doubled chromosomes is called a chromatid. During the first meiotic division, the homologous pairs of replicated chromosomes separate into two daughter cells. During the second meiotic division, the sister chromatids of each chromosome separate. **Encyclopædia Britannica, Inc.**

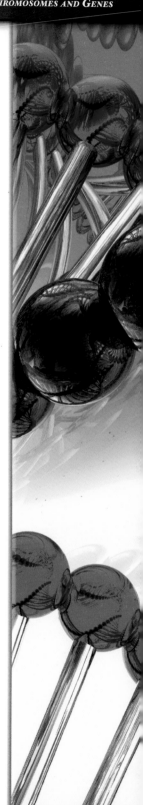

final result is four daughter cells, each with a haploid chromosome number. When a male gamete combines with a female gamete during fertilization, the diploid chromosome number is restored.

GENES AND THE GENETIC CODE

As arbiters of body form and organ function, genes must operate with precision. Each gene contains a biochemical code for the synthesis of a protein. The fundamental component of a gene is DNA, a nucleic acid made up of two strands of biochemical units called nucleotides. Each nucleotide consists of a phosphate, deoxyribose (a sugar), and one of four nitrogen-bearing bases: adenine (A), guanine (G), cytosine (C), or thymine (T). Chemical bonds connect bases on one strand with bases on the other, forming base pairs. The molecule resembles a ladder with the two DNA strands for "sides" and chemical bonds forming "steps." The nucleotide ladder winds around itself, forming a double helix.

When extra copies of DNA molecules are needed—as might occur before cell division—the molecule undergoes replication. In this process the two DNA strands separate—that is, the "rungs" of the ladder

How DNA Directs Protein Synthesis

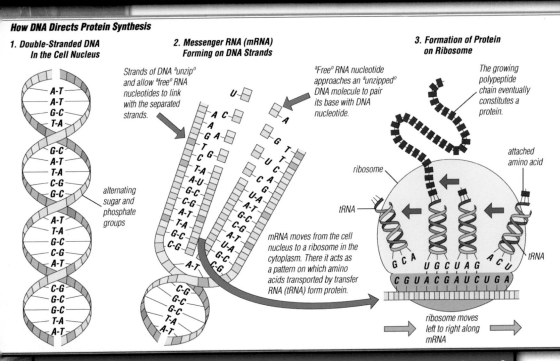

1. Double-Stranded DNA In the Cell Nucleus

2. Messenger RNA (mRNA) Forming on DNA Strands

3. Formation of Protein on Ribosome

Strands of DNA ºunzipº and allow ºfreeº RNA nucleotides to link with the separated strands.

alternating sugar and phosphate groups

ºFreeº RNA nucleotide approaches an ºunzippedº DNA molecule to pair its base with DNA nucleotide.

The growing polypeptide chain eventually constitutes a protein.

attached amino acid

ribosome

tRNA

mRNA moves from the cell nucleus to a ribosome in the cytoplasm. There it acts as a pattern on which amino acids transported by transfer RNA (tRNA) form protein.

tRNA

ribosome moves left to right along mRNA

DNA in the cell nucleus carries a genetic code, which consists of sequences of adenine (A), thymine (T), guanine (G), and cytosine (C) (Figure 1). RNA, which contains uracil (U) instead of thymine, carries the code to protein-making sites in the cell. To make RNA, DNA pairs its bases with those of the "free" nucleotides (Figure 2). Messenger RNA (mRNA) then travels to the ribosomes in the cell cytoplasm, where protein synthesis occurs (Figure 3). The base triplets of transfer RNA (tRNA) pair with those of mRNA and at the same time deposit their amino acids on the growing protein chain. Finally, the synthesized protein is released to perform its task in the cell or elsewhere in the body. Encyclopædia Britannica, Inc.

are broken. Each freed strand then serves as a template from which a new strand is produced. After the new strands are completed, each bonds to its particular template strand.

ESSENTIAL AMINO ACIDS

Although more than 100 different amino acids exist in nature, only 20 are found in living things. This latter group is called the essential amino acids. Some essential amino acids have more than one triplet codon. For example, the triplets AAA and AAG both code for lysine. Proline has four codons—CCA, CCT, CCC, or CCG—while tryptophan has only one: TGG. Three triplets do not code for any amino acid. Instead, they signal when transcription should be stopped. These three triplets—TAA, TAG, and TGA—are known as stop codons.

This produces two new DNA molecules, each consisting of one "old" strand and one new strand. This method of replication is known as the semi-conservative model. It is a key factor in the stable transfer of genetic traits from one generation of cells to the next.

Equally important for cell and organ function is ribonucleic acid (RNA). This nucleic acid is markedly similar to DNA except for three key features: RNA consists of a single strand (except in some viruses); in RNA the nucleotides contain ribose instead of deoxyribose; and base uracil replaces the thymine found in DNA.

The Human Genome

The entire genetic blueprint of an organism is called a genome. The genome contains the full set of genetic instructions for making all of the molecules that constitute the organism. In the case of humans, the genome is composed of more than 3 billion base pairs of DNA. These pairs have been copied and passed on letter by letter with gradual modification and expansion for more than a billion years since life began.

The human genome, like the genomes of all other living animals, is a collection of long molecules of DNA. These molecules are maintained in duplicate copy in the form of chromosomes in the nucleus of every human cell. They encode in their sequence of bases (A, G, C, and T) the details of the molecular and physical characteristics of the organism. The sequence of these molecules, their organization and structure, and the chemical modifications they contain also provide the genome with the capability to replicate, repair, package, and otherwise maintain itself.

In addition, the genome is essential for the survival of the human organism. Without it, no cell or tissue could live beyond a short period of time. For example, red blood cells, which live for only about 120 days, and skin cells, which on average live for only about 17 days, must be renewed to maintain the viability of the human body. It is within the genome that the basic information for the renewal of these cells, and many other types of cells, is found.

The human genome is not uniform. Except for identical twins, no two humans on Earth share exactly the same genomic sequence. Further, the human genome is not static. Subtle and sometimes not-so-subtle changes arise with startling frequency. Some changes are neutral or even beneficial; these are passed from parent to child and eventually become common in the population. Other changes may be harmful, resulting in reduced survival or decreased fertility of the individuals who harbor them; these changes tend to be rare in the population.

DNA forms the control center of the cell, directing the synthesis and activity of RNA, which in turn directs the synthesis of proteins. Sequences of paired DNA bases form a genetic code of 64 triplet codons, each a sequence of three nucleotides that codes for an amino acid (DNA). The sequence of amino acids produced from this code will form a particular protein. The code ensures that each protein is synthesized using the proper sequence of amino acids. A change in the DNA sequence causes the wrong amino acid to be added to the protein. In some instances this has no major effect; however, in many cases the change causes severe problems, ranging from birth defects to cancer or death.

CHAPTER 3

GENETIC DISORDERS

Diseases that arise from abnormalities in the genetic material are termed genetic disorders. Many genetic disorders are apparent during infancy; others are not evident until adulthood. Genetic disorders may result from mutations, or changes in the DNA sequence, of a single gene or defects in an entire chromosome. Most genetic disorders are multifactorial, resulting from the interaction of several genes coupled with environmental factors.

Couples in which either partner has a family history of genetic disorders or belongs to a high-risk population can benefit from genetic counseling. Prenatal screening is recommended for pregnant women who have been exposed to radiation or certain drugs early in pregnancy.

SINGLE-GENE DISORDERS

Single-gene disorders are caused by one or more mutations in a single gene that prevent its proper function. These disorders are

divided into two main groups, depending on whether the trait is carried on the autosomal or the sex chromosomes.

AUTOSOMAL DISORDERS

Autosomal disorders may involve dominant or recessive traits and can produce multiple abnormalities. The terms *dominant* and *recessive* refer to patterns of inheritance and gene expression. Autosomal dominant disorders result when offspring inherit an abnormal dominant gene from one parent and a normal gene from the other. (Inheritance of the mutant gene from both parents is usually incompatible with life; in most cases the offspring dies in utero or soon after birth.) Marfan's syndrome, an autosomal dominant connective tissue disorder, affects the skeleton, eyes, and cardiovascular system. Achondroplasia, a type of dwarfism characterized by abnormal trunk and limb proportions, results from a defect in the cartilage gene. The severe tremors, muscle twitching, and dementia seen in Huntington's disease are caused by degeneration of neurons in the part of the brain that controls movement.

Sickle-Cell Disease

Sickle-cell disease is a hereditary disease that destroys red blood cells by causing them to take on a rigid "sickle" shape. The disease is characterized by many of the symptoms of chronic anemia (fatigue, pale skin, and shortness of breath) as well as susceptibility to infection, jaundice and other eye problems, delayed growth, and episodic crises of severe pain in the abdomen, bones, or muscles. Sickle-cell disease occurs mainly in persons of African descent.

The "sickle," or crescent, shape of the red blood cell on the right is characteristic of sickle-cell disease. Shutterstock.com

46

Sickle-cell disease is caused by the inheritance of a variant hemoglobin gene from both parents. A person who inherits the sickle-cell gene from one parent and a normal hemoglobin gene from the other parent is a carrier of the sickle-cell trait. Most persons with the sickle cell trait have no symptoms of disease.

An estimated 1 in 12 blacks worldwide carries the sickle-cell trait, while about 1 in 400 has sickle-cell disease. If both parents have the sickle-cell trait, the chances are 1 in 4 that a child born to them will develop sickle-cell disease.

Autosomal recessive disorders occur when two copies of a mutant recessive gene are inherited. Cystic fibrosis is an autosomal recessive disease in which a single mutation causes thick mucus to build up in the lungs and airways, producing severe respiratory problems. In Wilson's disease, a defect that impairs copper metabolism causes toxic levels of copper to accumulate in the liver and brain.

Inborn errors of metabolism are autosomal recessive disorders caused by mutations in genes coding for metabolic enzymes. Phenylketonuria (PKU), which leads to severe mental retardation, is one of the few such disorders that is treatable: infants can

be tested for it, and brain damage can be avoided with a special diet.

Some cultural groups have a high incidence of certain autosomal diseases because of long-held customs of intermarriage within the culture. As the mutant gene is passed down through generations it becomes more common within the group. Tay-Sachs disease, which results in paralysis, dementia, and death by the age of five, occurs almost exclusively in descendants of Eastern European Jews. Sickle-cell disease, a disorder caused by a defect in hemoglobin that affects oxygen transport in the blood, is most common among people of African descent. The thalassemias, a group of hemoglobin disorders that cause mild to severe anemia, are fairly widespread, though the highest prevalence is among people from Cyprus.

SEX-LINKED DISORDERS

Genetic disorders caused by mutations in genes on the sex chromosomes (X and Y) are called sex-linked disorders. Human females have two X chromosomes, one inherited from each parent. Males have one X and one Y chromosome: the X chromosome comes from the mother and the Y chromosome from the father. Genes for most sex-linked

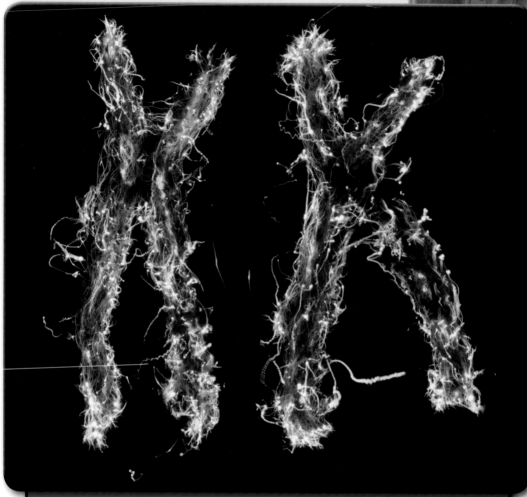

This is a photographic image of a healthy pair of XX chromosomes.
Lawrence Lawry/Photographer's Choice RF/Getty Images

disorders are located on an X chromosome.
Females rarely inherit two defective X chromosomes; females with a defective gene on
one X chromosome are protected from its

effects by the normal gene on the other X chromosome but have a 50 percent chance of passing the defective gene on to their offspring. Sex-linked traits are expressed mostly in males, because they have only one X chromosome. Hemophilia, a sex-linked blood-clotting disorder, is observed almost entirely in males. Duchenne muscular dystrophy is a sex-linked disorder that affects males beginning in early childhood.

CHROMOSOME DISORDERS

Chromosome disorders occur from structural defects in the chromosome or from having too many or too few chromosomes. Down's syndrome, the most common chromosomal disorder, occurs in persons with an extra chromosome 21. The syndrome manifests in infancy and is characterized by intellectual disability, small skull size, slightly slanted eyes, and a short neck. Less visible characteristics include heart defects and a high incidence of acute lymphocytic leukemia.

Sex chromosome disorders occur in both males and females. Females born with only one X chromosome develop Turner's syndrome, characterized by a short, blocky physique and lack of sexual development.

FORMS OF DOWN'S SYNDROME

There are three forms of Down's syndrome. The most common form is trisomy 21, in which all of an individual's cells contain three, as opposed to two, copies of chromosome 21. The extra chromosome is a result of random, abnormal events in cell division that occur during embryonic development or during the development of egg or sperm cells. The presence of the extra chromosome in cells gives rise to the signs and symptoms of Down's syndrome.

In mosaic Down's syndrome, a rare form of the disorder, only some of an individual's cells contain a third copy of the chromosome. Because there are some cells that retain the normal 46 chromosomes, certain aspects of the disorder, such as intellectual disability, are not as severe in people with mosaic Down's syndrome relative to people with trisomy 21.

The third form, translocation Down's syndrome, occurs when the extra chromosome in the 21 pair breaks off and attaches itself to another chromosome. Translocation Down's syndrome is the only form that may be inherited. A parent who possesses a balanced translocation—a chromosome rearrangement with no extra genetic material from chromosome 21—can pass the translocation to an offspring. Carriers of balanced translocations

do not have signs or symptoms of the disorder. Mothers carrying a translocation have a 12 percent risk of transmitting the genetic rearrangement to their offspring, whereas fathers carrying a translocation have a 3 percent risk of transmission.

In Klinefelter's syndrome the male has two X chromosomes and one Y chromosome, resulting in small genitals, lack of sperm formation, late puberty, and, occasionally, breast development.

MULTIFACTORIAL INHERITANCE DISORDERS

The single largest class of genetic disorders are the multifactorial inheritance disorders. These result from the interaction between mutations in several genes and drugs, radiation, viruses, or other environmental factors. Some of the most common birth defects—including congenital heart disease, spina bifida, cleft lip or palate, and pyloric stenosis—are multifactorial. Such common conditions as cancer, heart disease, Alzheimer's disease, and diabetes are now considered to be multifactorial disorders

Cleft lip and cleft palate are among the most common multifactorial birth defects. **China Photos/Getty Images**

with a genetic component. Because of the multiple factors involved in these disorders, the pattern of inheritance in families is less clear than that observed for single-gene and chromosomal disorders.

CHAPTER 4

THE PRACTICE OF GENETIC ENGINEERING

Almost every living cell holds a vast storehouse of information encoded in genes. The artificial manipulation of one or more genes to modify an organism is called genetic engineering.

The term *genetic engineering* initially encompassed all of the methods used for

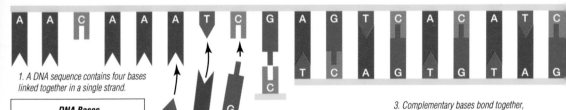

1. A DNA sequence contains four bases linked together in a single strand.

DNA Bases

adenine A ◀ T thymine
guanine G ▬ C cytosine

2. Complementary bases join together following base pairing rules.

3. Complementary bases bond together, forming a double-stranded molecule of DNA.

DNA contains two strands of nucleotides linked together by chemical bonds. Each nucleotide contains a phosphate, deoxyribose (a sugar), and one of four nitrogen-containing bases: adenine (A), guanine (G), cytosine (C), or thymine (T). The bases of one strand are linked to bases of the second strand. Because of their structures, adenine can only pair with thymine, and cytosine can only pair with guanine. Encyclopædia Britannica, Inc.

modifying organisms through heredity and reproduction. These included selective breeding, or artificial selection, as well as a wide range of biomedical techniques such as artificial insemination, in vitro fertilization, and gene manipulation. Today, however, the term is used to refer to the latter technique, specifically the field of recombinant DNA technology. In this process DNA molecules from two or more sources are combined and then inserted into a host organism, such as a bacterium. Inside the host cell the inserted, or foreign, DNA replicates and functions along with the host DNA.

HISTORY OF GENETIC ENGINEERING

Genetic engineering had its origins during the late 1960s in experiments with bacteria, viruses, and plasmids, small, free-floating rings of DNA found in bacteria. A key discovery was made by Swiss microbiologist Werner Arber, who in 1968 discovered restriction enzymes. These are naturally occurring enzymes that cut DNA into fragments during replication. A year later American biologist Hamilton O.

A Controversial Technology

Recombinant DNA technology has produced many new genetic combinations that have had great impact on science, medicine, agriculture, and industry. Despite the tremendous advances afforded to society through this technology, however, the practice is not without controversy. Special concern has been focused on the use of microorganisms in recombinant technology, with the worry that some genetic changes could introduce unfavorable and possibly dangerous traits, such as antibiotic resistance or toxin production, into microbes that were previously free of these.

Smith revealed that one type of restriction enzyme cut DNA at very specific points in the molecule. This enzyme was named type II restriction enzyme to distinguish it from type I and type III enzymes, which cut DNA in a different manner. In the early 1970s, American biologist Daniel Nathans demonstrated that type II enzymes could be used to manipulate genes for research. For their efforts Smith, Nathans, and Arber were awarded the 1978 Nobel prize for physiology or medicine.

The true fathers of genetic engineering were American biochemists Stanley Cohen and Herbert Boyer, who were the first scientists to use restriction enzymes to produce a genetically modified organism. In 1973 they used type II enzymes to cut DNA into fragments, recombine the fragments in vitro, and then insert the foreign genes into a common laboratory strain of bacteria. The foreign genes replicated along with the bacteria's genome. Furthermore, the modified bacteria produced the proteins specified by the foreign DNA. The new age of biotechnology had begun.

Werner Arber celebrates with his wife after receiving the 1978 Nobel prize for physiology or medicine. **Keystone/Hulton Archive/Getty Images**

How Genetic Engineering Works

The action of restriction enzymes—also called restriction endonucleases—is the crux of genetic engineering. These enzymes are found only in bacteria, where they protect the host genome against invading foreign DNA, such as a virus. Each restriction enzyme recognizes a short, specific sequence of nucleotide bases in the DNA molecule. These regions, called recognition sequences, are randomly distributed throughout the DNA molecule. Different bacterial species make restriction enzymes that recognize different nucleotide sequences. By convention, restriction enzymes are named for the genus, species, and strain designations of the bacteria that produce them and for the order in which they were first identified. For example, the enzyme *Eco*RI was the first restriction enzyme isolated from the *Escherichia coli* (*E. coli*) strain RY13.

Recognition and Cleavage

Of the three types of restriction enzymes, type II is the most useful in genetic engineering. Types I and III restriction enzymes cleave DNA randomly, often at some distance from the recognition sequence. By contrast, type II restriction enzymes cut DNA at specific sites within the recognition sequence. Each time a particular restriction enzyme is used, the DNA is cut at precisely the same places in the molecule. Today more than 3,600 type II restriction enzymes are known, forming a molecular tool kit that allows scientists to cut chromosomes into various desired lengths, depending on how many different restriction enzymes are mixed with the chromosome under investigation.

BLUNT AND STICKY ENDS

At the cleavage site, different restriction enzymes cut DNA in one of two ways. Some enzymes make incisions in each strand at a point immediately opposite another, producing "blunt end" DNA fragments. Most enzymes cut the two strands at a point not directly opposite each other, producing an overhang in each strand. These are called "sticky ends," because they readily pair with complementary bases on another fragment.

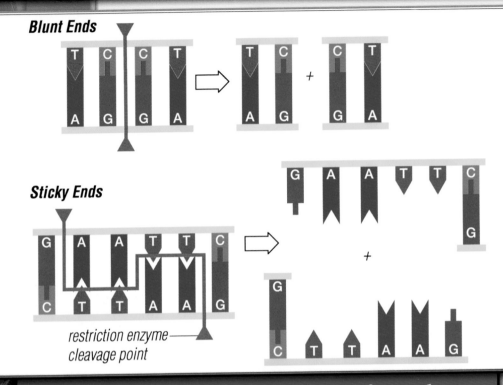

Blunt Ends

Sticky Ends

restriction enzyme
cleavage point

DNA sequences can be cut in two ways. One type of cut produces two DNA strands with blunt ends; that is, there is no overhang on one strand or the other. A second type of cut produces two strands with sticky ends; because of the site of cleavage, each strand extends beyond the complementary region of the strand pair. The ends are not actually sticky. Rather, the term denotes that the overhang allows these fragments to bind more readily with other strands. Blunt ends are more difficult to join. Encyclopædia Britannica, Inc.

RECOMBINANT DNA TECHNOLOGY

Genetic engineers use restriction enzymes to remove a gene from a donor organism's chromosome and insert it into a vector, a

enetic Engineering of Recombinant DNA

Molecule A

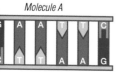

restriction endonuclease cleavage point

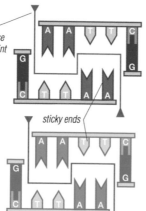

sticky ends

Recombinant DNA

Molecule B

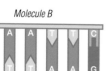

digest molecules with same restriction endonuclease, EcoRI

separated strands are mixed with enzymes that seal the sticky ends, forming a recombinant DNA molecule

Recombinant DNA is formed by using a restriction enzyme that cuts the double strand at a particular point. The same enzyme is used to cut a second piece of DNA. When the fragments are mixed together, the complementary ends of each strand will bind with those of the other, forming a recombinant DNA molecule. Encyclopædia Britannica, Inc.

molecule of DNA that will function as a carrier. Plasmids are the most common vectors used in genetic engineering. These are circular DNA molecules found in some bacteria. They are extrachromosomal molecules, meaning that they replicate independently of the bacterial chromosome.

The first step in the process involves mixing the donor organism's DNA with a set of restriction enzymes that will isolate the gene of interest by cutting it from its

chromosome. In a separate step, a plasmid is cut with the same restriction enzymes. The donor gene DNA is then spliced into the plasmid, producing a recombinant DNA (rDNA) molecule that will function as a vector, which is introduced into bacterial cells. Inside the host cells, the plasmids replicate when the bacteria replicate. Because this produces many copies of the recombinant DNA molecule, recombinant DNA technology is often called gene cloning. In addition, when the bacteria's DNA initiates protein synthesis, the protein coded for by the inserted gene is produced.

CHAPTER 5

APPLICATIONS OF GENETIC ENGINEERING

Because genetic engineering is a relatively new technology, scientists are still exploring its wealth of potential applications. Three areas that have already seen important developments resulting from genetic engineering are medicine, industry, and agriculture.

GENETIC ENGINEERING IN MEDICINE

Medicine was the first area to benefit from genetic engineering. Using recombinant DNA technology, scientists can produce large quantities of many medically useful substances, including hormones, immune-system proteins, and proteins involved in blood clotting and blood-cell production. Before the advent of genetic engineering, many therapeutic peptides such as insulin were harvested from human cadavers and the pancreases of donor animals such as pigs or horses. Using foreign (nonhuman) proteins

A worker operates the distilling and extraction apparatus at an insulin factory in 1946. Before genetic engineering, most insulin used to treat human patients was taken from the pancreases of pigs and cows. **Chris Ware/Hulton Archive/Getty Images**

posed serious risks: in some patients the introduction of foreign proteins elicited serious
allergic or immune reactions. Furthermore,
there was a great risk of inadvertently transmitting viruses from the donor tissue to the
patient. By using human DNA to produce
proteins for medical use, such risks were
greatly decreased, if not eliminated.

INSULIN AND OTHER THERAPEUTIC PROTEINS

The first genetically engineered product
approved for human use was human insulin.
Insertion of the human insulin gene into bacteria was accomplished by the pioneer genetic
engineering company Genentech. Following
extensive testing and government approval,
large-scale production of genetically engineered human insulin was carried out, with
recombinant human insulin first marketed
to diabetics in 1982. Today, genetically engineered human growth hormone, parathyroid
hormone, and similar proteins have provided
a new standard of care to individuals suffering from endocrine diseases.

The interferons also were among the
first recombinant proteins produced for
therapeutics. Interferons belong to a class

Genentech, founded in 1976, was the first company to make use of the then revolutionary technology of genetic engineering. Justin Sullivan/ Getty Images

of immune-system proteins called cytokines and are used to treat viral infections and some cancers, notably the virulent form of Kaposi's sarcoma common in patients with AIDS. Before the advent of genetic engineering techniques, it took laborious processing of thousands of units of human blood to obtain enough interferon, of somewhat impure quality, to treat a few patients.

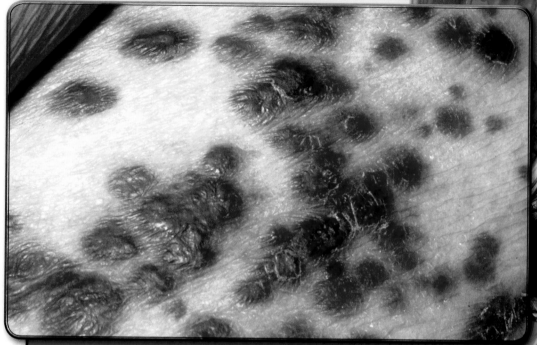

The cancer called Kaposi's sarcoma can be treated by interferons. These immune-system proteins are produced naturally by the body and can also be made through genetic engineering. **Kallista Images/ Collection Mix: Subjects/Getty Images**

Genetic engineering enables the cost-effective production of vast quantities of very pure recombinant interferons.

Recombinant technology is used to produce a wide range of therapeutic substances. These include cytokines, interleukins, and monoclonal antibodies, all of which are used to fight certain viruses and cancers. Critical blood factors are now mass-produced through

recombinant technology; these include clotting proteins such as factor VIII, used to treat bleeding disorders such as hemophilia; erythropoietin, which stimulates red blood cell production and is needed to combat anemia; and tissue plasminogen activator, a protein that helps dissolve the blood clots that block arteries during a heart attack or certain types of stroke.

Vaccines

Genetic engineering has also provided a means to produce safer vaccines. The first step is to identify the gene in a disease-causing virus that stimulates protective immunity. That gene is isolated and inserted into a vector molecule such as a harmless virus. The recombinant virus is used as a vaccine, producing immunity without exposing people to the disease-causing virus.

Diagnostics

Recombinant DNA technology is also used in the prenatal diagnosis of inherited diseases. Restriction enzymes are used to cut the DNA of parents who may carry a gene

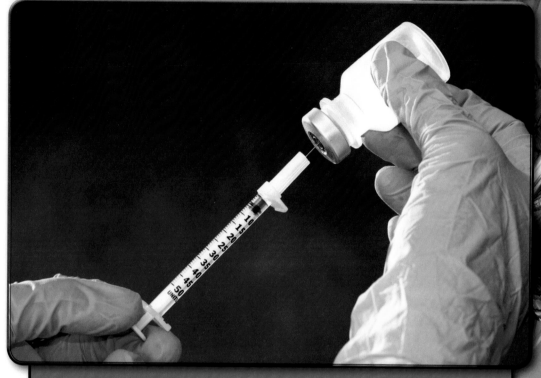

Vaccines are much safer thanks to genetic engineering. Hemera/ Thinkstock

for a congenital disorder. These fragments are compared with DNA from the fetus. In many situations the disease status of the fetus can be determined. This technique is used to detect a wide range of genetic disorders, including thalassemias, Huntington's disease, cystic fibrosis, and Duchenne muscular dystrophy.

69

Gene Therapy

In gene therapy, scientists use vector molecules to insert a functional gene into the cells of individuals suffering from a disorder caused by a defective gene. Vector molecules containing a functional gene are inserted into a culture of the patient's own cells, which then deliver the inserted genes to the targeted diseased organs or tissues. The most commonly used vectors in gene therapy are viruses. In the target (human host) cell, the virus "unloads" the inserted gene, which then begins functioning, restoring the cell to a healthy state. Another method is to take a cell from the patient, use recombinant technology to remove the nonfunctional gene and replace it with a functional one, allow the cell to replicate, and then infuse the engineered cells directly into the patient. For example, to treat the life-threatening deficiency of the immune system protein adenosine deaminase (ADA), scientists infuse cells from the patient's own blood into which researchers have inserted copies of the gene that directs production of ADA. Although there are still a number of challenges to overcome in developing gene therapy, it remains a research area of great promise.

GENETIC ENGINEERING IN INDUSTRY

Genetic engineering has been especially valuable for producing recombinant micro-organisms that have a wide variety of industrial uses. Among the most important achievements have been the production of

Polyester thread is fed into an embroidery machine. The process of making polyester involves genetically engineered microbes. Kim Steele/The Image Bank/Getty Images

modified bacteria that devour hydrocarbons. These microbes are used to destroy oil slicks and to clean up sites contaminated with toxic wastes. Genetically engineered microbes are used to produce enzymes used in laundry detergents and contact lens solutions. Recombinant microbes also are used to make substances that can be converted to polymers such as polyester for use in bedding and other products.

GENETIC ENGINEERING IN AGRICULTURE

The use of recombinant DNA in agriculture has allowed scientists to create crops that possess attributes that they did not have naturally and that improve crop yield or boost nutritional value. Such crops are termed genetically modified organisms (GMOs). By manipulating plant genes, scientists have produced tomatoes with longer shelf lives and pest-resistant potatoes. Genetic engineering has also been used to

"Golden rice" is a nutritious type of white rice that has been supplemented with beta-carotene. **Joel Nito/AFP/Getty Images**

boost the nutritional value of some foods. "Golden rice" is a variety of white rice to which the gene for beta-carotene—a precursor of vitamin A—has been added. This nutrient-dense rice was developed for populations in developing countries where rice is a staple and where vitamin-A deficiency is widely prevalent.

CREATING GMOs

The ability to obtain specific DNA clones using recombinant DNA technology has made it possible to add the DNA of one organism to the genome of another. The added gene is called a transgene. The transgene inserts itself into a chromosome and is passed to the progeny as a new component of the genome. The resulting organism carrying the transgene is called a transgenic organism or a genetically modified organism (GMO). In this way, a "designer organism" is made that contains some desirable trait.

Genetically modified organisms are produced using scientific methods that include recombinant DNA technology. Encyclopædia Britannica, Inc.

Genetically modified organism

insecticide gene created
using recombinant
DNA technology

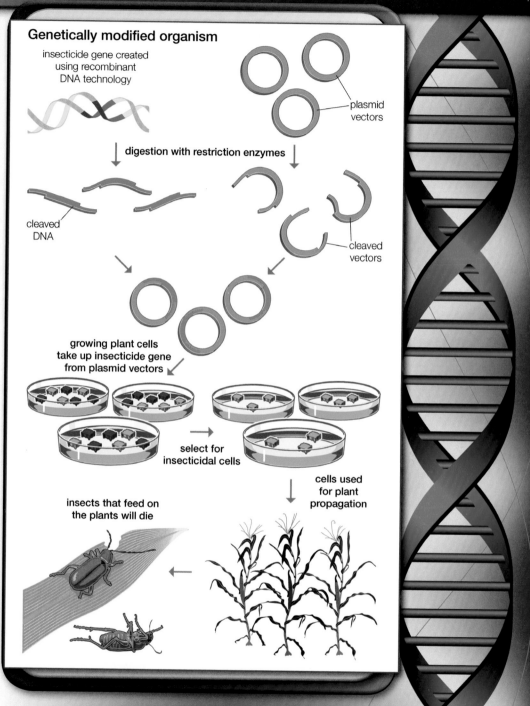

plasmid
vectors

digestion with restriction enzymes

cleaved
DNA

cleaved
vectors

growing plant cells
take up insecticide gene
from plasmid vectors

select for
insecticidal cells

cells used
for plant
propagation

insects that feed on
the plants will die

The practice of producing genetically modified organisms is not without controversy. Some government agencies and ecologists, as well as numerous consumer groups, have voiced serious reservations about the safety of such organisms and the products produced using them. While many of these objections have merit, it is unlikely that the use of genetic engineering in agriculture will be halted. Although GMOs are banned in some countries, the vast majority of the soybeans, cotton, and corn raised commercially in the United States are genetically modified.

Genetic research has come a long way since Gregor Mendel's groundbreaking experiments of the late 1880s. Later landmarks included the discovery of the structure of DNA in the 1950s and the introduction of recombinant DNA technology, or genetic engineering, in the 1970s. Genetic engineering now dominates genetics and can be said to represent the culmination of more than a century of research in the field. Because the focus of all genetics is the gene, the focus of laboratory geneticists is to isolate, characterize, and manipulate genes—the goals of genetic engineering. Ongoing research will no doubt produce new genetic combinations that are of value not only for their scientific interest but also for their uses in medicine, agriculture, industry, and other fields.

GLOSSARY

allele Any of two or more forms of a gene that in combination control a specific trait (e.g., eye color or blood type).

amino acid Any of 20 different kinds of molecules that link into long chains to form proteins.

autosomal disorder A genetic disorder caused by a mutation on a non-sex chromosome.

chromosome The microscopic, thread-like part of the cell that carries hereditary information in the form of genes.

codon A set of three adjacent bases on a DNA or RNA chain that codes for a specific amino acid in the production of proteins.

diploid Consisting of two sets of chromosomes, or double the haploid.

DNA (deoxyribonucleic acid) A complex molecule that exists inside the nucleus of every cell and is the fundamental component of genes.

dominant Describes an allele that has greater influence than its partner allele for a given trait; the less influential allele is called recessive.

filial generation A generation in a breeding experiment that is successive to a

mating between parents of two distinctively different but usually relatively pure genotypes.

gamete A mature reproductive cell that contains one set of unpaired chromosomes (i.e., the haploid number) and combines with another gamete from the opposite sex during the fertilization process.

genome The sum total of all the genetic material of an organism.

haploid Consisting of a single set of chromosomes, or half the diploid.

heterozygote An organism that has two different forms of a certain gene, one inherited from each parent.

homozygote An organism that has two identical forms of a certain gene, one inherited from each parent.

monohybrid cross A mating of two parents that differ in only one trait.

nucleotide A string of organic molecules composed of a nitrogen base linked to a sugar and a phosphate. Nucleotides are the basic structural units of DNA and RNA.

phenotype All the observable characteristics of an organism, such as size, shape, and color, that result from the interaction of the genotype with the environment.

recessive Describes an allele that fails to express itself in an observable manner because of the greater influence, or dominance, of its opposite-acting partner allele.

somatic cell One of the cells of the body that compose the tissues, organs, and parts of that individual other than the reproductive cells.

Canadian Institutes of Health Research
    (CIHR)
160 Elgin Street, 9th Floor
Address Locator 4809A
Ottawa, ON K1A 0W9
Canada
(613) 941-2672
Web site: http://www.cihr-irsc.gc.ca
Comprising 13 "virtual" institutes, the CIHR
    funds research on many health prob-
    lems. The researchers in its Institute
    of Genetics are dedicated to advancing
    understanding of genes and the human
    genome as well as social and cultural
    issues surrounding genetics.

Genetic Information Research Institute
    (GIRI)
1925 Landings Drive
Mountain View, CA 94043
(650) 961-4480
Web site: http://www.girinst.org
Founded in 1994, the GIRI seeks to under-
    stand the processes that affect the
    genomes of various organisms.
    It maintains a database of repetitive
    DNA sequences from the genomes of
    many species.

McGill University and Génome Québec
    Innovation Centre
740, Dr. Penfield Avenue
Room 7104
Montreal, QC H3A 1A4
Canada
(514) 398-7211
Web site: http://gqinnovationcenter.com
The McGill University and Génome
    Québec Innovation Centre conducts
    research in the field of genomics (the
    study of genomes) and proteomics (the
    study of proteins within genomes). It
    also offers genetic services, such as
    sequencing and genotyping, to members
    of the scientific community.

J. Craig Venter Institute (JCVI)
9704 Medical Center Drive
Rockville, MD 20850
10355 Science Center Drive
San Diego, CA 92121
(301) 795-7000
Web site: http://www.jcvi.org
The JCVI takes a multidisciplinary
    approach to genomics-centered research
    and has been at the forefront of scien-
    tific discovery. Its DiscoverGenomics!
    Science Education Program offers

opportunities for development for both students and educators interested in bringing genomics to the classroom.

National Human Genome Research Institute
National Institutes of Health (NIH)
Building 31, Room 4B09
31 Center Drive, MSC 2152
9000 Rockville Pike
Bethesda, MD 20892
(301) 402-0911
Web site: http://www.genome.gov
The National Human Genome Research Institute at the NIH conducts biomedical research related to all aspects of the field of genetics. Resources for students include fact sheets, an Online Education Kit, and career guidance for those wishing to pursue work in the field of genetics.

WEB SITES

Due to the changing nature of Internet links, Rosen Educational Services has developed an online list of Web sites related to the subject of this book. This site is updated regularly. Please use this link to access the list:

http://www.rosenlinks.com/biol/gene

BIBLIOGRAPHY

Claybourne, Anna. *The Usborne Introduction to Genes & DNA* (EDC Pub., 2006).

Fridell, Ron. *Genetic Engineering* (Lerner, 2008).

George, Linda. *Gene Therapy* (Blackbirch Press, 2003).

Hayhurst, Chris. *Looking at How Genetic Traits Are Inherited with Graphic Organizers* (Rosen, 2006).

Johnson, R.L. *Genetics* (Twenty-First Century Books, 2006).

Kidd, J.S., and Kidd, R.A. *New Genetics: The Study of Lifelines* (Chelsea House, 2006).

Schafer, Susan. *DNA and Genes* (Sharpe Focus, 2009).

Snedden, Robert. *Cell Division and Genetics*, 2nd ed. (Heinemann Library, 2008).

Walker, Denise. *Inheritance and Evolution* (Evans, 2010).

Walker, Richard. *Genes & DNA* (Kingfisher, 2003).